THE GEORGIA POETRY PRIZE

The University of Georgia Press established
the Georgia Poetry Prize in 2016 in partnership
with the Georgia Institute of Technology, Georgia State University,
and the University of Georgia. The prize is supported by the
Bruce and Georgia McEver Fund for the
Arts and Environment.

SOUTH FLIGHT

SOUTH
FLIGHT

Jasmine Elizabeth Smith

THE UNIVERSITY OF GEORGIA PRESS

Athens

© 2022 by the University of Georgia Press
Athens, Georgia 30602
www.ugapress.org
All rights reserved
Designed by Erin Kirk
Set in ITC New Baskerville
Printed and bound by Sheridan Books
The paper in this book meets the guidelines for
permanence and durability of the Committee on
Production Guidelines for Book Longevity of the
Council on Library Resources.

Most University of Georgia Press titles are
available from popular e-book vendors.

Printed in the United States of America
22 23 24 25 26 P 5 4 3 2 1

Library of Congress Control Number: 2021947316
ISBN: 9780820360904 (paperback)
ISBN: 9780820360911 (ebook)

To my father for leaving;
my mother for staying.
For the state of Oklahoma,
which is both my exile and home.

*I acknowledge that the land which I write of and call home
is the original and continual traditional territory of Caddo,
Wichita, Pawnee, Quapaw, Osage, Apache, Kiowa,
Comanche, Arapaho, and Cheyenne.*

*I acknowledge and recognize my responsibility to the
original and current caretakers of this land, water and air,
including the thirty-nine tribal nations who dwell in the
state of Oklahoma and all of their ancestors and
descendants, past, present, and future.*

Contents

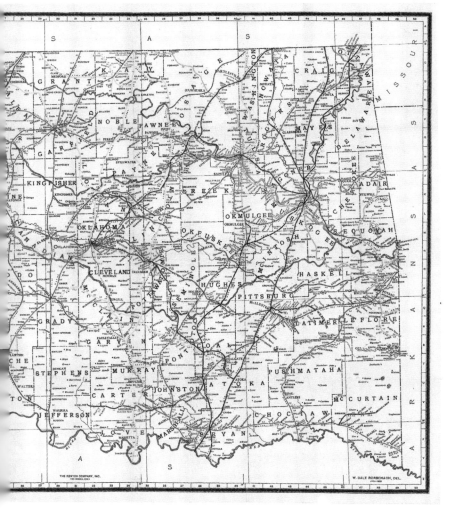

Dale W. Rorschach, *Railroad Map of Oklahoma*
(Corporate Commission of Oklahoma, 1920).

I'm feeling sad and lonely
and there's a reason why.
Because I've been mistreated
I wish that I could die.
All you've ever brought to me was sorrow.
That's why I'm leaving here tomorrow—
'Cause I'm tired of grieving and make-believing
Over someone whose heart's just like iron.

"I'm Going Away Just to Wear You Off My Mind"
~ Alberta Hunter

Blacktown Blues of Oklahoma

My tongue survival of rag holler.
My teeth spoon metals
stronging my ache sundown. Lord
let this song mine cross
some darkened lengths. Gospel call it little
candle. Let sounds I make
lamp pitch and lighten
ears of those who cup
Atlas-canning jars to back doors.
Tongues of dust turn my heart bowl.
I be first to admit this ain't no gospel,
but might my song, simple
it may be, choir doves up yard,
quicken Oklahoman air prairie.
I pray my eyes wring witness,
twenty-one freshwater routes
against forgetting this home
I call South.

Jim Waters Makes Parable of Seed

March 13, 1921

what remains of blacks through these parts
ain't much. soil loam. even seeds
refuse to peel melon rinds.
we pressed hard. just to see us run.
forgive me. b.
this frankness. I know you
rather talk scripture: the hijacked
price of sugar. how to set seething
broilers for sauce. but even in eden,
eve come to know what she wasn't—
sweetness of flesh. bitterness
of pits taught her no
such thing as the call of paradise
birds in exile of clasped wild.
b, you'd have me
play your minister. pray something
sprout out our stalk. tell me what
happens when your hope for me
sprawls big as south,
yet this kind of living make me
smaller than a few chickweed seeds?

Beatrice's Prayer to Be Reborn in the South as an Old Cypress

April 21, 1921

Sometimes I pretend I'm made of a sturdier thing—
cast iron, good work boots, your papa's plough
summer he pulled cut
through fields on his own back.
Wide waisted, an old cicada cypress
can't be rounded by belts or gingham dress ties.
A cypress tree does not fail in an ice storm
or when wind spools
the North Canadian River over
every crop and front porch,
does not tell of secrets: termite, wood
ear, the skirmish
of broadcloth skirts, your lovin
hands, or who hangs, face near
and looming like ripe casket fruit among the web
worms. Even your trapper blade can't cut
the heart or the ugliness we've come to know,
for what it's worth, much less our names. Jim—

—*Beatrice Veredene Chapel*

Beatrice Repents on the Behalf of Nature

Preacher say reckon the wayward.
Children warned good measure 'bout a blues
woman. Unclean, she who worships
the body, sings herself soft
into back rooms. Best to wary the barnyard
sounds & songs heifer as her jaw
grows & shrinks accordingly
to the many breeds of hunger.
Even yet, more cussin,
her legs spread in sharp
key for any who will eat. Jim.
I used to be a church-
going woman. Rolled my nylons
beforehand so they wouldn't run
at the knees. Used to button
the collar of my Sunday
best. Now, I ribbon
cape jasmine to my bridge,
undress the steel
stride of your quick hands.
Their scale—my ruin.

[Greenwood Ghosts Dress Their Sunday Best]

After Gwendolyn Brook's "We Real Cool"

this no parade for your pleasure

no one winds up brass band
stand celebration

this no market we knife
melons sample

or haggle down our price:

aspirin, lady-hand
leather of Louise half heels,
Bit-O-Honey, salted seeds

from Ferguson Drugstore
& Grier Shoemaker.

up here, no one hunch their backs,
low eyes, pantomime themselves
minstrel or maid

we don't give—

we grand

stand our own
streets

headlining Tulsa Star's
Newspaper,

Attorney Spears, Saddler & Chappelle.

we call Lazarus up from the dead,

bluebonnet gurney in
Frissell Hospital's basement.

just seen to be seen we filled
out, we bright enough, we gold

end weed, we oil reserve, we keep

no time, we Bunn's Shoeshine
gospel. we holy

spirits
broken from the mouth
& matchstick
Bethel Adventist Church pews.

past Abner & Hunter
Barbershop, Carter Billiards—

Hardy Furnished Rooms,
Dixie Theater—

you mistake our procession for ghosts,
envious, the figurative

you claim we isn't.

so why you stop & stare?

is our beauty so vain it a form
of resistance?

[Jim Imagines a Drink with Lead Belly after the Lynching of Lloyd Clay]

My husband was a hardworking man
killed a mile and a half from here.
His head was found in a driving wheel
And his body hasn't ever been found.
—"In the Pines" ~ Traditional American Folk Song

take a seat boy. drink that you might hear me. songs
all stories. & what story depends on who in the room.
white men might stir their fingers a little bit. lighten themselves
with two dimes from their wallet or a water-weakened deal.
their girls might loosen hands to shorten up their skirt hems.
tap a patent toe to tile. might even feel wild,
a calico of string plucked foreign & bucking
in their belly. i isn't saying they wrong. but them folks
always off beat to our kind of holler. my black girl never slept
in no pine. it the cruel needling of white folks
keep her cold. when i sing it,
my girl never dance nicely
to this song. & when i say her husband killed,
i mean lynched. thousand men couldn't stand
to see that boy go on with his kind of goodness.
when i say his body never found, i mean he gotten rid of
in the worst of ways. no wet roll lodged in river
mouth nor he hung from tree, a treaty
flag his girl might washboard in widowing. he very well
might been soaked in coal oil, disowned
by his people, his girl, a song. isn't a trace left.
in this bridge of southern blues,
he's been all swallowed up.

Beatrice Interprets a Night Terror

May 3, 1921

What good a dream if I can't interpret it?
Each card I pull, a reversal. Something bound
to be ill fated these days. Jim. What it be?
My mind turned ill & folks mean?
What window broken pane?
What rock thrown rose? Who next to be found
washed up in the deformation of rivers dead?
How I've taken to washing my clothes colored—lynching
black—half part my misery & the rest:
oak galls, rust of nails, iris roots & walnut shells.
Should I martyr my unkind thoughts?
I can't seem to trust, no one, no thing, but this here mine.
& if things be different, I'd be dumb as asters, blue-
eyed-charlocks, ironweeds. My heart be an open plain
for you—
               & for me, I'd grow endlessly.

Jim Recalls the Soldier He Once Was

We return. We return from fighting. Make war for democracy.
We saved it in France, and by the Great Jehovah, we will save it in
the United States of America or know the reason why.
—"Returning Soldiers" ~ W. E. B. Du Bois

truth was I wasn't ever much of a soldier.
never knew how to straighten a shot. kick-
back scared me. folks in my hometown used to joke
I couldn't even wet my hands with bloody knots

of catfish guts tackled in beaver's bend.
honestly. made me cry.
stomach of their throats & mouths teeing open.
my hands soft, but I'm quick
as the arkansas river, moonlight,
cicada music of storehouse dives & old
folks who still dream upstream of siblings
gone missing in mississippi cotton bolls.

training down in fort still, I'm ashamed
to admit I was scared to use my gun.
other soldiers push me around.
call me sissy, a flower picker
faceup tasting the trench. ask if I

even belonged in the service.
these days even the songs on the radio sound
tired as me. courage & bravery
simply the static catchline of songs,
their chorus, a boy whose back breaks
like vowel in misstep of a grenade.

I'm a musician, collapsing
my tongue against the promise
of a soft woman
wearing only stockings back home.
her delight, a badge I pin to my lapel.
no right in any of this.

back then, I carried my gun like a steel guitar.
my fingers hard as iron tacks, listening hard
for the life I had to take fore it took mine—
each shot, a slide to warp notes flat.
just like a song. & like I said.

no one right in any of this.
I'd tried my hardest to fight this war
as a field holler. I called out—

> but this nation gave me no
> response.

Beatrice Contemplates the Wild Dog Killing Prey

June 1, 1921

Yesterday, under scuffed moon
a few wild dogs   hungry
followed the trail of prey miles over.

Through basin bottoms, arsenic roots, past waterline—
What they willing to do satisfy
hunger—mouth yolk soft young
in nest & chew the rock
of their wrists into spoons?

Jim. You claim war
is fought on every storefront
threshold, train track, bitumen state
line. You say men

must break hands, articulate
their bodies into weapons.
Yesterday them dogs tore

through Greenwood, Oklahoma.
The break of back dimity & small, shared
between multiple mouths—   town   burned
ground.

& this constant
sharpening, what of it?
What of children? What of women? What become
of me? Hold me near. I bare
my neck & belly

to your livid teeth. I ruin sweet
spire & oak leaf, poultice
them to eyes   I might
become blind.

Love Letter on the Eve of Revolution

I am all of wanting. only blues
seems to make sense these days—

to touch you like parted
vowels from harp teeth. I can't breathe;

therefore, I am greedy for passage
of air: clarinets cleared of cold

coughs & low-down tonk
house songs slapped out my anger.

how can a strangled chord
progression picked in love

sound like something other
than violence? how might I chorus

hornets into sonnet
when my mouth feels

a containment? my tongue stiff,
an unsoaked reed, I keep

tryin to play every undigested place
of our existence but my tongue

so dogged out, even my notes flatten cruel.
will I draw or blow lovestruck, the fermata

between your eyes & parting braids—
head northbound without turning back?

b. I beget you what little I still have:
my body throaty, a staged pathos,

at 2 am, the trombones' bent
melodies & riot of beaten drumskins.

of honest folks, this world makes
sinners' ramblin. I know this blues

sounds mean,
but how can I love on bended knees?

Beatrice Begs Jim to Pull Out Her Bad Tooth

You mistake my body as gladness,
concavity, a spitting wet grin.

My mouth a cavity, a bleeding slice

airing crowns
of rot & scrap-metal abscesses.

Nothing sweet exits it or goes in.

Rinse of salt & cloves, I apply—
To anesthetize, beg your hands, two pliers

to master my mouth a numb bloody organ.

I garnish you, sewing red threads
from every bedroom door handle.

Each time you enter, you pull out—

Soon I'll be toothless & without bite.
A token denturing your jaw.

What is better? To keep

on aching or a milk-gutted mouth
incapable of its own sound?

Freedmen Ghosts Make Preparations for Juneteenth

June 16, 1921

after the emancipation called three years too late,
we rode the central flyway far as brazoria, texas,
like droves of swallows. some of us strong,
others just plain exhausted of dying.

dead now
one way or another, those who sought paradise
came to curse length of lousiana's border
for believing within stolen land
lay Black folk's piece & not price of equity.

how you supposed to go on when all you feel
is tarrying the church prayer circle
or burning down the streets?
we wish we could let jubilee rise
like creek water in our throats.

that which is blessed,
we ain't tryin to lay to ruin.

we all know y'all desperate for any slip
of joy these days,
that you don't starve yourself out of livin.

but we can't give you a seat at this makeshift table.
the one where y'alls humiliated funeral hats tipped
just so it don't show the grief slapped red
in the whites of your eyes
& the emancipation we dreamed
for future lives.

Jim Writes His Marriage Vows

August 15, 1921

marriage don't sound like a streamer of tin bells
cut from canned white fish or a cup
of white rice. ours a different kind,
& this an august wedding you will wear
lace but no good-luck blue to.
clear the broom, sleep the same
bed, claim to have, but I just can't
seem to hold.

beatrice. last night, I named it a proposal,
your ring finger used to cork
a half-drunk bottle of corn rye.
when loosened to drink ourselves back
to that celebratory rot of sleep, the bruise
of band hitched you my sundown

wife. I said this our first dance, a makeshift
tune of lonely steels & bickering
box strings. each our heels scuffin salt-pork
raw against all our stepping on the other.

beatrice. can never tell if it just this dance
or fury as we wipe the royal icing
of pig shit from our wedding dress
in disappointment of bed, work & yard. *I do*

know our grief. *hereto,* beatrice vernadene chapel,
from this day forward, for better, for worse—
your bouquets bound. my vows elegiac. I *promise*
you wrong & wrong don't make right.
woman. us can never say we do.

[Jim Imagines the Ghost of Robert Johnson at the Cross-Roads]

y'all good folks tarry nightlong
for every bottle-
necked bootlegger chew bad
tobacco, call his weeping
want of moon-
shined women
the tuning key of blue.

it easier to swallow hell
than a body
hanged down highway side.
how it easy to say I part ghost
cus' my own low down doin'.

what bed I cuckolded? for my soul,
how much I wagered: a fool's
gold record deal, my face
cutting newspaper back pages, my need

to enter front doors? what drive
my back into corners,
devil or dread, I was never
mine to sell. what crossroads I dared
pass over in the first place?

Beatrice Advises Fathers When Jim Makes Way to Crossroads

When he comes to town, your girl warn.
Tell her hold her breath, count
    backward
ten till he out her sight.

              Bible shame & pray the blood
        don't run her out of pure
        -thread stockings, church
        slip, your home.

        Backhand her
best not sling them eyes doe or quilt
colored ribbons through her hair
wax. Jim might not be a righteous, but lord
knows a suggestion
              when he sees one—
How henbit dart an ear
or dress taken in. Even her *hello*
    suckles sanded
horehound & slices of oranges. Papa—
double-fold them covers. You'd better
caulk his draft from your old door
    'cus when he enters,
            he stomps tracks

    on floorboards & bleed
        bathwaters red.

No matter how much your girl rinses,
it as if she let a trap
    blade reopen her right up.

Jim Recalls His Birth as a Wasp

October 24, 1921

mama's pain my birthright—
stung by wasp month fore she found
she with child. I the ninth. she pray
I last turn her open river on bed,
clot milk silt, acre her breasts long.
I just another man's hunger she ain't got
means to feed. cursing

first breath, I came to blue, choked,
bedcover apple red.
been my experience, my blood ain't tender. too big
for any woman hold inside her.
pitched in afterbirth pail,
my spirit something far flung.

if I a man of sight, I'd sense
my troublin way back then.
& if I a peddler of porch herbs,
pinch this, mouth full of that—I'd give
my mama a swig of love, sweeten
what sufferin spit out.
make her moonshine, no man,
dead or alive, swell her to feelin. a wasp

isn't no bee. don't sacrifice
hurtin others. beatrice. I whole hives—
jealous tenfold my eyes, wings pinch
back pin cushion, if I don't take off—
that my mama crushed that wasp
with back of hand, better yet left me slice
backdoor air where I belong.

How to Break a Generational Curse (& Other Lessons my Grandmother Has Taught Me)

Never fall in love with a slave owner—
everyone always moving
to the ownership of somebody else.

Never deny love to another.

Even if you are broken, remember
you are only yours to give.

Always put a little dirt under your tongue—
'cus God blessed it & it one of the few things
that don't hurt.

Never own a gun—

colt, carbine & remington bullet,
you your most powerful weapon.

Walk in arms & in pleasure,
drink but never consume in excess.

May you never cut your flesh
unless it an act of survival
or beauty.

Never make a deal out desperation.

Be wary of medicine & men
in armchairs who call themselves holy philosophers.

May you never consume poison.

Never take someone else's name
lest your ghost become their burden
& theirs yours.

Speak your dead by name.

Even though you are a woman, you stand
on your own two feet.

Leave home forever but remember
who you come from.

Never leave without a fight, but never out stay
your welcome.

Destroy & create in the same right
hand.

Keep your eyes & your ears open.

On your behalf,
never let someone speak, but always listen
closely to what enemies your got to say.

Don't start nothing, but honey finish
everything come your way.

[Father's Ghost Sees Jim Waters Off
at the Santa Fe Railway Station]

when you finally leave, pack what little you have in case. cicadas
clockin up your call time. out east in Cherokee County, twisters spin
spools of air. lowland, heifers & prize hogs rub
the scent of storms rising sheet glass tall. reckon by tomorrow
someone else be dead. pocket your grief
& trapper blade you fork dirt clots into scissored wings
of flycatchers, sliced your lover's breasts in route
of the Santa Fe ticket line. a woman's blood be a parable
of freedom on this side of the color line. go on now. take
yourself. take the prairie-fire trees. take the sorghum seeds & the lard
crock for your hardness & time. take her heart. boy. survival
ain't the same as stealing.

Weeping for Spilt Milk
An Interlude

Trouble, trouble, I've had it all my days.
Trouble, trouble, I've had it all my days.
It seems that trouble's going to follow me to my grave.

"Down Hearted Blues" ~ Bessie Smith

Ils M'ont Nommée la Marinière

I ran away from St. Louis, and then I ran away from the
United States because of that terror of discrimination, and that
horrible beast which paralyzes one's very soul and body.
~ Josephine Baker

Child, I don't claim to be a mariner or anything of the sort.
Remember the time I buoyed up, half dead on the banks of the
Mississippi River—slipped in thinking I'd retrieve treasure in
some mud. I was resuscitated by the Delta and, once revived, sang
blues—water drowned, carnations fauceted from the throat of
dumped bodies.

I ain't never learned to swim well, and like a dumbstruck girl
walking the shore who imagines rows of sunken ships, flooded
towns intact, and gold tureens stuck in the heels of rock and reef, I
still stick my hands into every new body of water. See what I might
pull from their tide: kelp, bird nest, heart valve, cold, shell, and
even though I try not to, your bottled letters from back home.

> I hope Paris treatin you good—
> Round here, things just seem
> to keep on gettin worse.
> You still sing those songs
> we love so much?

I don't claim these legs since leaving have learned to tread any kind
of ocean. Today, on stage, I appeared as one who walked on the
Atlantic, the salt hot on my calves in the ear of water. My song was
all paddling upset. And how them Parisians hollered. Called me
winged gull, Venus Negress, light as oil, *ils m'ont nommée la marinière.*
But what the water obscures—the turning of ocean nettle, sea glass,
the broken hull of a body as a boat. As I cried out in finale, the
waves all but lifted me up.

For Phillis Wheatley at Water's Edge

I.

The sun slumbers in the ocean's arms.
No. Today just gray, implacable
on pleated currents. Salt builds
the timber moors, the bow
of a boat.

Poetess, there was a time
when you might have walked
freely upon the ocean's edge,

imagined what lay across
its legato'd indigo
note. In Williamsburg,
which John will braid leash
of ribbon into your hair?

How you look
to your reflection, its shoaling
of Atlantic. You are sickened

by the pet of it. *Sweep*
the surface. Make billows roar.
How you wish your mouth
a typhoon on the overlook
these foreign waters.

How you wish two cackling waves
of your hands, to drown
the cargo of your tongue.

II.

In vain my Eyes explore the watr'y reign.
How these waters have never been
your home. Nevertheless, you are slave
to write of them. Your letters worked
to graphite voyage lines.

How waves on waves devolve without end.
In this place, you are never asked what it is
you miss of home. You can hardly remember—
T'was not long since I left

                                    my native shore. you recall
                        only ocean & mother, the meter
                            of jaundiced, belched eye
                                    whites, sore
                        scrubbed, your foreign
            tongue, an iron coffle, the bait
                of blood, the *anxious breast*
                        pitched over-board at first
                                                light.

III.

Astonish'd ocean feels the wild,
uproar. How you've grown tired
of this subject of water. How it too European, diatonic,
ugly un-uplift. Unnatural, this desire
                        to shift continents,
            unspool entire peoples
                into the bevy of sea—their thirst
                of boundless power & work of war.

Phillis. Does a whip cut one of your many tongues?
After the board of slave ship, you are pen named.
Yet, they scratch their heads. Ask why
must you compose a thing carnationed
                    drowning, backwards?

What *glorious toils you write.*
In Williamsburg, you are not allowed
to sit, drink
pekoe tea, or wish
to be dead, until every emotion is recited.

          The refluent surges, beats the sounding shores.

This talent masters attempt
                    to mast.
Yet, you are the eye
of the storm, writing yourself a *glorious toil.*
How they read
but do not navigate
          the shawled hurricane—

                              your tongue.

Indigofera

The slave's deadly contact with the fermentation and lye application
process that transforms the plant (indican $C_{14}H_{17}O6$) into the
commodity dye (indigo $C_{16}H_{10}N_2O_2$), rendering it an exchangeable
product that can be given measurable and nominal value in dollars.
—*In the Clearing: Black Females Bodies, Space, and Settler Colonial
    Landscapes* ~ Tiffany Jeannette King

I want the indica color that built up
plantations from swamplands—
my hands blued
in vats of boiled water cuffed to yards
of anil-steeped cloths. To hold its hues,

I must carry the thick sputum of dye
from water
to the scalded wringing of death
in the outlet of fields.

Big as mayhaw berries, horseflies hang
low, lick the rot of lye
smoke and seethed stems, reminding me,
I must be careful to not keep my hands
submerged for too long. History,

as indigo clutches fast,
clots poisonous in the pores and cuticle beds.
It must be cleared like lead
wort, dead red nettle, forget-me-nots
and the roots of a thousand and one Atlantic crossings—

> *the mutiny of heteroglossiac utterances, cyan*
> *tongued underdeck. God's language*
> *is foreign both on sea and inland,*
> *consonants gold clicks and vowels English.*

What we no longer hear or care to know—
how sharks once followed the salted blood
bolts of boats across the ocean.

From the Southern Slave Medical Companion

For worms, eat sugar-laced
drops of turpentine in the afternoon.
And for your general wellness drink

tinctures of horsemint and wild
sage. To quit cravings for dirt, longings for home,
clamp the red of your tongue with a clothespin
so it don't come loose from wash line.

Bleed and cup your temples for grief
and fits of apoplexy. To cuts, both visible,
and them yet be seen, apply vinegar

wet cloths. To purge many
unwanted thoughts, dose bitter
peach tree bark taken
by spoonfuls every hour.

To prevent pregnancy, lay motionless—

hold brass pins, six copper
coins under your lip as he takes
his fill. Consume gunpowder,

pellets of birdshot
mixed with milk for nine days.

For unwanted pregnancy, chew the root
of cotton plants. But if you do,
and that baby still born

pray mercy   *mercy*   *mercy*

and avoid them beds
of sick houses at all costs.

Mulatto

To be mixed is to have
my mama's eyes and hair.
It is the pale woodblock cut
from my papa's blood.
I admit he could've passed
if he wanted
and that he was born octooned
between the color
lines of The Rex Theater
and the midnight showings of Louise Beaver's
Life Goes On.

What I don't say
is that when he was born,
my great granddaddy didn't let
my grandmamma bring him nowhere near
his house lest she track prints of dirt
onto good house carpet.
She was told to take off

her shoes, wash her hands
of that whitish baby nursing
the corner
of a cardboard box in the Buick's backseat
while headed toward orphaned
New Orleans dressed in wiry crochet
and new booties. To be half
isn't always a Loving story.

Let me set the record straight.
This isn't a southern retelling
I scrub my family up Creole.

Someone didn't love
my grandmamma
but her skirt and body
spread against pavement
like a pat of margarine, her size

three penny loafer lost
in Rudbeckia, dandelion wet
bobby socks, grosgrain ribbon fisted
from her French braid. Mulatto—
quadroon—octoroon—mixed—
is often to be carved in half.
These things my kind don't recount.

Drowned & Reborn

after Clyde Woods's *Development Drowned and Reborn*

when the lower 9th Ward levee broke
back in 1961, we prayed
we might become the slipknot of black
water snakes. & because we had no hands,
our venomous bites fastened
      bayou rocking our babies, fettering
      them to pirogues, our fugitive bodies
      safe in maroon of *cipriere.*
& because we no longer had homes,
      we took shapes of swamp
      gulls, scavenging
      the officers' badges,
      fortified what was left
      of our altering nests—
      driftwood, plastic,
      the bloated bodies
      of idling government vans.
that year, the watershed
reached over four feet on Claiborne Avenue in Tremé—
fourteen in the parishes of St. Bernard & Plaquemines.
hundreds us became alligators,
      belly crawling the muddy velvet
      bowl of Bayou St. John
      when prices of bottled water,
      gas & canned meats rose.
& because we had no tongues
to speak, our rows
of teeth grew longer, sharper
with expression. some say, we ate
      what remained of our dead,

our hunger desperate. imagine our opening
mouths, our chorus-snagged
jaws, devoid of song—
how a dirge might sound to some a kill.

Bodies Seen at or Disposal Sites: *In Lack of Carnations*

after *Computations as to the Deaths from the 1921*
Tulsa Race Riot by Richard "Dick" Warner

In Newblock Park City Incinerator on the East & West Ends.
Buried in Booker T. Washington, Rose Hill, Oaklawn
& Black Perryman Cemeteries—

Somewhere in Jenks, tossed in a river & buried
in a sandbar. Under the railroad bridge over the Arkansas
River. In Standpipe Hill, Reservoir Hill, North Cinnati Hill—
Mohawk & Chandler Park areas.

On the 11th Street Bridge, burned.
On the Katy Railroad tracks, burned as well.

Hidden in the Brady Theater basement,
on East 36th & South Peoria,
between South Peoria & Riverside Drive on 41st Street,
between East 31st & East 41st Street & South Lewis.

Entombed in the mines:
on NW corner of East 21st Street & South Sheridan,
on NE corner of East 21st Street & South Yale,
on SW corner of East 21st Street & South Harvard
& all along East Apache.

Placed under other railroad tracks,
in the fairgrounds under the Reserve
building on East 15th Street. In a hole &

tossed in other mines—the ones in West Tulsa,
south of Collinsville, between Catoosa & Claremore.
Bodies seen passing Oneta on the Katy Rail-Road train
& along the tracks west of Oakland Cemetery.

Disposed on the pier west of Tulsa on West 3rd
between Tulsa & Sand Springs in the hop clover & wild violets.
Rumors of mass graves near Crystal City in Red Fork,
on way to Sapulpa, Tracy Park across from SW corner of Oaklawn,
under the Traffic Circle at Mingo Road & East Admiral . . .

All are disposed in mass
graves
of nonhistories.

Historic White DET653

Who wouldn't want to be painted in such a way?
For hands, two feverish doves of acrylic.

A mirror or virgin form of apple for body.
In wash of turpentines and ammonias, baptize me.

I don't have much. Yet, I can pay for this commission
with my suffering, my silence,

my death.
When I emerge from cleaning dish will Indigo

and Mississippi Red be released from ferrule of brushes?
Will I be symbolic? My throat painted a garland

of carnations, birdcalls, your unsight of my mothers,
kept me out of the gallery reconsidered?

Zouzou

Ain't of no kind word in what they've been telling you.
Heard they call you Songbird these days. Part your beak
and collar the long part of neck with sapphires.
When are you going see
you aren't ever goin be one of them? Don't mean a thing
they pour Prosecco in porcelain dishes.
Let you lap leftovers from their palms.
Do they pinch your sides to regurgitate the slug of white
cake, candied roses, the baked breasts of hummingbirds?
Merchant the fetid smell of it into crystal?
I heard their trade isn't much different
from what is done here at home. Only difference
is they prefer their Black rare and chilled over ice,
fine caviars knifed from the ovaries of the South.
Maybe at night you prowl the Turkish rugs,
dressed in Schiffli lace, an ankle ribbon tagging
you rare specimen? Do they call you beautiful
for one of your kind? Pocket your songs
and measure your skin for couture?
And for who do you think it will make
statement when you worn to the Grand Palais Garnier?

My head goes round and around
since my baby left town.
I don't know if the river's running up or down.

"Moonshine Blues" ~ Ma Rainey

Correspondence from Chicago, Illinois, to Boley, Oklahoma

When Israel was in Egypt's Land,
oppressed so hard they could not stand.
Let my people go.
—"Go Down Moses" ~ Black Spiritual

Postmarked ~ February 22, 1922

lord woman. sometimes you were too bright,
& I had to squint to recall the undone shape
of that land, how the plough failed
to rail cut for seed. the metal dulled
when struck with stone. during the wet months,
the thatched roofs of our tenet home leaked
as your wanting of me. beatrice. weren't no pail or washtub
big enough to hold that kind of end.
in your midst, how a man keen to forget
even the dirt floors of his place
belong to someone else. your song heavy
on me, twice, I almost forgot my daddy's name.
waters, was the only thing my people knew
of the state of oklahoma through the parting
of field songs after emancipation.
little we knew, rivers
only drag red mud—no moses. what remains
won't soon be black in them parts.

—*Jim Waters*

Correspondence from Boley, Oklahoma, to Chicago, Illinois

Postmarked ~ March 19, 1922

Jim, we all know the story of Brer Rabbit
Molasses and Apple Jack
spooned by capful to cure a whooping cough.
Best double layer to keep from catching cold
in the wet months. I claim our ache
isn't one old wives' medicine, flight, or prayers
can shake. It rained last night. Bottomlands
all racket as the strike of water forced
vibrato on corrugated steel roofs like a hundred
metal mallet strokes of spoon bellies against the thigh.
Hackberry and locust trees broke
as if they'd ever stood upright in the first place.
You finally flee that terror you claimed?
Or like this weather there is no break in it?
Just keeps on and on, cast down, cutting
as you rush toward that loud and ratty stride
of a northern city. Sometimes, I want
nothing more than disaster,
this mud-land due for cleansing
in wait of some word, death, letter.

> *Just one letter, Jim.*
> *I'm not asking*
> *that much—*

and Jim. How all them blackbirds clap wet wings
after rain, their necks breaking from beaks bowled,
fat with water even after taking flight.

> *Jim, I'm asking—*

IV

Now I can read his letters;
I sure can't read his mind.
I thought he's lovin' me;
He's leavin' all the time.
Now I see my poor love was blind.

"Crazy Blues" ~ Mamie Smith

Black Town Blues: Greensborough, Oklahoma

Postmarked ~ June 19, 1922

When I taught to hold myself tightly bound, black
bird all tressed up, arm length in twine.
Tell me pretty. Jim. How I able, up & just fly?
Each my arms nails, siding strays of storm loosened shutters.
Church sisters claim, my manners good as canned oranges.
Teach me, why I to hold this double bind of blackness tightly.
These days, I got potential to be an impeccable church picnic.
Drowned in baptismal waters, sisters say I born of new spirit.
Tell me how I able? You just up Jim, away fly prettily?
To battering of beds, I wear muslin gloves, seam my mouth prayer.
Lower my eyes to cut of well-known killings.
I teach myself not to hold blackness but bind my mouth tightly.
Starched white hoods tent revivals; congregating round cross
all is burned upon open holy ghost fires.
Tell me. Am I able & just?
When I a bird tressed up in this black bible length of twine—
When God is man, think he both storm & light—
How to lift careless wing when you taught not to hold
       yourself
or nothing for that matter? Tell me Jim. It isn't
       even got to be pretty.

    How I to sing
    my way out
    this bible belt?

            How out this bible,
            I belt
            my own way?

Beatrice Forges Jim's Love Letter

July 5, 1922

offer me a glass of cold water, tea,
or some other sweetened thing
if you got it.
I'd like it if you'd wear that dress
I like best. the one
with all them buttons. each eyelet
my fingers press close like eyelids.
through each cut, I touch
the clean skin of your back.
how, these days, I got no need
for the stronger stuff. how the taste
of you slaps the back my throat
like bathtub-water gin & strong horn leads.
leaves me breathing through teeth, my tongue
a reed in want of you. sundown, when I come
knocking at your door, I stagger
my hands across dresden quilts,
through the cursive of slip straps,
spilling the inkwell where stockings'
elastic seam meets your thighs.
how I unpin
your hair, all done up,
wishing to make of you my bottle or fan
flower field. beatrice. let this
bedroom be a harvest. don't talk
about the sorrowful things: the black
dog pacing the yard, the boys
who hang like wash in myrtle trees, the dead
ballot, what we lack or where
we should be getting.

Beatrice Reads the Almanac to Forecast the Growing Season

Postmarked ~ July 17, 1922

Almanac warns of brass kettle
summer. A bust, even the roots
of wild grass chokin on red dirt.
Hasn't rained in a stretch, almost long the time
it took you to concoct flight. Not by oriole or rose

-breasted grosbeak but in the passenger car
of the Sixth Line, cutting up the topsoil
of the Illinois border as if by metal wing.
But Jim, what does a man like you care
about the condition of weather? All this

small talk. You've never had an ounce
of kindness for this land. Your hands soft
as cotton flowers, catch cold when they meet
spade, rake, pickaxe, South, or shackle.
Cough and call sick,

your throat tricks, played black-eyed,
for a thing too hard. The yams and rice
will be undone. Soon, pulled for fire.
Thrown out like yarn needled poor
from cast stitch. Jim. This where you
and I differ. When slipping

beneath card skirt, or easy money,
your hands find persistent song,
something of sorghum and sundown sweets.

Jim—a growing season like most things in a life

like ours is predicted to fail. Women don't
get the privilege of running away.
Used to taking a tool, calling a stone
a ready green seed. You like bird
migrate to the long shadows of Sear's iceboxes.

Ask, B, *where's my bed?*

[Boley Ghosts Haunt Jim]

when them fools from pretty boy floyd's crew came on up in here flashing
their teeth & pistols like knife marks of american shad in light-casted
water, silica faking jewels of altus rocks, lord knows, they had another
thing coming. suppose they thought they the first of their kind try to take
advantage of—rattlers cocking their mouths toward field mice. thought just
because we a town founded on the hands of black women, they got stake to
our mares, mortar & money. but ain't that a dyin shame when the weak go
on to persist the strong? whole town gathered outside farmers & merchant
bank with bird guns & squirrel rifles after mccormick killed birdwell—sure
they was just cheap outlaws fattened up on the paper's spotlight—but we
imagined shooting up the heart of the confederacy to tatty white funeral lace.
& how they wore that ugly dress. this is what we know. we dodge ill will
every day. if given chance, we be upturned so fast—all us wind up being
kindling for someone else's fire:

greenwood & sulcom;
rosewood & ocoee;
elaine & sprinfield;
Beatrice & Jim.

Beatrice Visits the Church

Do not grieve for the joy of the Lord is your strength.
~ Nehemiah 8:10

Postmarked ~ September 8, 1922

I tell myself, time and time again—
Beatrice. There is always so much
be put up round here. Thickening upon a twice-rinsed dish,
ringworms of grease itch my supper spoons.
Even my bedroom floors rashed
with dirt. Somedays, I barely got

the strength to move this mess or dress myself
for church. These days grief has become a location:
chewing at mud and current, the upper acre
Red River steam liners hunger for, my scrap
rug comfortable before its cookstove, all South.

How these days folks complain how I come to care
little for the concerns of others. What the front page says,
mothers clawing black hats and dress
fronts mute in the streets, what boy is vested
in barbed wire, or what lack of coffin is lifted upstream.
Frankly said, I just unconcerned with using loss
as a tool. Tired of planting. Just plain tired
of clearing a path for folks.
You ever feel the satisfaction of not tending to,
withholding to lick your own welts
of milkweed with keresone?

Sunday and the preacher man preach.
As with folks, it's all about what they take—
the pass of an offering plate and how much I am

willing to give. *Beatrice, why you don't light a paraffin prayer*
for all them poor souls. You are blessed among women.
Hoarding the tithe of my pennies until poor,
I swallow the communion of wax;
all rubbed, I an outed candlewick.

Beatrice Imagines Ida Cox Pays Her a Visit at Her Dressing Vanity

I've got a disposition and a way of my own.
When my man starts kicking,
I let him find another home.
—"Wild Women Don't Have the Blues" ~ Ida Cox

Girl. Wipe them tears or the good Lord will
really give you something to cry about.
Been my experience when you deny
how anybody able, he takes, just to remind
of all we got. You fine enough lookin
& decent person easy enough to find.

In times of trouble, call upon a half mixture
of talcum powder & hazel water to lift
the puffiness from your eyes, fresh hyacinths,
a bottle of gin, song to invoke the patron saint
of runaways & railways. Harriet Tubman

the first blues woman anyway. Could have cried
a lifetime when iron knocked the chorus roll
into her head. What she was given,
she used instead: a set of teeth to bite
relief into bullet, hands to wring weakness
from runaways whimpering in dark acres.
Dare those backs turn at border. Go

iron this messy dress, shine up these patent shoes.
You still got ears to hear heaven, a mouth to sin—
Why not use them both why still you is still able?

Remember your mama wounded
for anything she might call her own: your vanity
table, ribbon for hair, a breast full of glass
buttons, a corner of sugar cake to soften a new kind
of song within her. Honey. I isn't saying break

don't hurt, but it a simple fact this world beat you
down, black eyes like jet, stricken you blue.
Beatrice. Will you hang
your head or find a way all your own?

B's Ascension to Bee

Postmarked ~ November 23, 1922

A cold come off the Canadian River
& even bees sicken on December
driving my feet back into wool.
Between the teeth
of floorboards, in *Weibel* milk
bottles waiting porch, bees
collect like bullet casings
knowing this home of mine
a dying place. For days, in a row,
they lose their way
in cotton, patch & fence beans.

Ain't a single compass left among them—
bees hailing up my windows,
running my rooftop,
socks of coins split at the seams.

Jim. A woman of little waste
might hull the beads of dead
bees into decoration to wear in yard,
bed, while setting something to boil.

She to hope, she might become
something of flight
finding the broken beautiful.
In her best heirloom, drink
the insect wings handpicked
with thumbs of bottomland water.

She to believe that something placed
in her mouth makes it true—
hope, a man's ring finger, myth.

Ages ago, my folks believed women
like me could climb
air as stairs or even when slaves,
the briar & saw-toothed Wichitas to sky.
My people could fly.

I suppose, I believe in this too—
Believe, a bee, *B*, I become.

Beatrice & Gladys Bentley Discuss the Fortune of Livin Alone

Flushed with cash, before I forced to disown myself in front of the whole world, dream was I could buy out Madison Grant of his marble busts, convince the entire Harlem Tenderloin of his unphilanthropy. To white folks, charity always look like the throwaway crusts of some hand-me-downs. No good to snack or wear to Sunday school. When I was younger, I never one of them who out desperation to eat at the master's table played the nigger. I the kind to lift silver for when emancipation come & reallocate silverware to edify the entire block. Reparations come too late, so I took the entire damn plantation. Those days, it seemed I had my freedom, then some: comforts of Italian shoes, raw silk suits, my hair a flash flood under my gentleman's hat. Even my fists heavyweight champions of gold rings. & I had a look & song all my own—buttermilk in way of lovers come all the way up from New Orleans to feed me sugar cubes soften by gin & lick the space between my toes. But don't mistake this as an act of colorism. My girls were good girls. If I was the kind to have daughters, I suppose that what they would have been. Anyways, I wasn't no sharecropper, but with the well of my voice I was able to peel back the hardness of womanhood from each layer of their wet petals. There are far worse things than fawned father, lover, mother, sister, master. Back then, I was backpeddling the slave trade. I was their vessel; they my passengers. I was the passenger; they my vessel. Because there was no place in this world uncruel, it was certain we all would leap overboard.

V

Was a time you coulda' walked right in
& call this place your home sweet home;
But now it's all mine, for all time.
I'm free and livin' all alone!
Don't need your clothes, don't need your rent.
Don't need your ones and twos.
Though I ain't rich, I know my stitch;
I earned my strutting shoes.
There, hand me the key that unlocks my front door,
Because that bell don't read [*your name*] no more! No!

"Sam Jones Blues" ~ Bessie Smith

[Jim Imagines He & Charley Patton Pick a Boweavil from Backyard Chicago Crop]

a boweavil ain't much different from you, jim
hauled across state lines, wind hissin
you place to place. you brung nothing
but clothes on your back & a hunger so hooked
you blade 10,000 acres of Oklahoma cotton,
Chicago or Kansas City gray stones
in just a matter of years.
hack-jawed, a black man's work never done—
chew through ripen' cotton bolls, sundown
curfews, the heart of his woman. when farmers say,
why you pick my farm? i got respect for man
or thing got a little plague within them.
eat through a bushel of arsenic or sheared fist
with ravenous mouth. look white
men square in the eye when caught with a mouthful,
a parcel of land or cash. say, *i will eat. we will* eat no matter
if placed in keg of ice, when burned down to infested root.

Jim Waters Sweet-Talks Beatrice about the Paradox of Blackness, Our Good Lord & Gold

these days a better man I'm striving to be.
I found christ bereft of beauty up north—
     in stretch of sprawling asphalt.
every acre this city a way,
     even alleys & avenues tilled black by wall
street ethic. a proverb
can't keep me. & I isn't no fool—
     there is monies abundant,
knowledge & far more
     precious things.
my kin once speculated
sorghum & cotton by the pound—
     sharecropped only to bury
     a handful of our pennies into ground.
I isn't that. & you is
right. these northern negroes wrong
as juiced plums. isn't no shame
in the sweetness of what they hanker for—
     cash & mortared business fronts fatten
     ten-fold hopes within their hands.
madame c.j. walker, patron saint of paraffin & fat furs,
packages oil curl cream even in the grave. her pearl-knot
jokes the lynch. beatrice. kill me
with this kind of richness.
instead of penny can one change his name to gold?

Jim Writes Beatrice a Letter That Will Never Be Sent

dear beatrice,
sometimes, I scratch at the soft wedge
between my forefinger and thumb.
tongue side, a lie bump rises. you know
the saying. devil's braille go hand in hand
with no kind of goodness.
how the body of a man parse
wisdom: money getting soon, trouble,
someone to mess about his bed.
you hush girl. & don't take things
I say so serious. I just want you
to trust me, keep us, in my own
kind way. Somedays, I want
to lug sweet water by barrel
to your doorstep. by post,
send fat envelopes of doilies, a fistful
of smashed black clementines,
king oliver's brassy song
to play the pentecost
from your skirts. & other days,
I just want to fix the chime
of your throat. blue & wetting,
keep you full of me. b. I never claimed
to be much but my will & love
is another metaphor for land.
you don't know its value
until it cut into: what undergrowth
of water, alluvium, your bed
unwilling limestone & clay.
it unknown if man runs land
or it the land that runs him.

Beatrice Forges Jim's Admission of Guilt

April 1, 1922

in a new place, one must quickly grab on something familiar.
beatrice. remember, I've never been fond
of swimming—every time I jumped in, I clung to the lip
of rocks and drowning lines of blue-
grass. I was afraid roaming undercurrents would pull me under
if I was to let go. best navigate what you don't know
with clear sense of direction: a lover's
ripe smell, mouth sweet and swilled with whiskey,
the down beat of my work song. my hands
as they did never much cared what they grabbed in purchase.
that cattail as good as blue, b, and in these circumstances
the polyester dress slipped overhead just as good as yours.
no mind the price, don't you low
your eyes to my coming and goings. don't you think
of me that way. imagine us an uprising—everything done for good,
cost after cost, for the greater other.

—*Jim*

Jim Prays a Healing over B's Affliction

April 30, 1922

behind these plucked fingers
of chickasaw & tickseed
you accused me, I the one
sprung your braids heavy—
sifted you orb
weaving spiders in gifts
of flower spray.

claim you, I planted them
in your pillowcase to bite
& braille your ears.
in you, to web another bad
dream, worse than awful
state of these streets.

you say, I shook
the salt cedars,
where below you sat.
each brass-eyed ermine,
a kerosene bomb
leeching down.

my dear. it is 1922
& there are far worse things
than your plate-glass heart
I break over my hand.
south & greenwood are on fire,
enamel cup & summer red.
there is no second
thought to pull the gun
regardless of right or law.

another woman tucks
her accusation in handkerchief—
wicks its monogrammed trim
to tribune's headline.
in the burning mouth
of isopropyl, it flung through
our sitting rooms & streets.

& I know you needed me,
be your enemy. for these things
seemed too big. too many
for you to take on. it easier to bicker
the clementines & ground cherries
I smashed soft in love at your doorstep
than look upon this world
conditioned to break you & I
conditioned to break.

Correspondence from Boley to Chicago

Postmarked ~ January 16, 1923

I belong to you as much as I belong to him. That a palm full
of moonlight men hunt under. To survive as I do   a woman
must   straighten lips to a seam of metal   temper each part.
Keep her eyes   steeled to all the cast-iron cooking   feed
her red mouth   hungry   open & close   like climbing
columbines. Remember Jim. If you won't have me   another will.
Pretty stories of Wabash Avenue lifted   a hundred harlequin
pigeons   bawdy holler of rusted horns   won't ever put up
vinegar, sugar, crocks of lard on my shelves. Jim don't take
it personal. I throat the raw strip of the North   my want of
home. How I take   no promise from each   stay   of
your cool starched collars.

Correspondence from Chicago to Boley

Postmarked ~ February 13, 1923

there be many times I wanted to look back
but was worried it'd make spilled salt of me.
the drunks outside hotel lobbies
bull's-eye pigeon nests for sport,
throwing each into street & under boot
in order to hear their sickening
wet against washab avenue.
beatrice, if I a bird, I might twist on a wire,
show off the red rebar of my tongue in shrieking protest.
if I you, I might pick the shell from my heels,
yolk the pieces back together again.
but b, I'm just a man.
I've had a long day on the factory line.
it's a thirteen-block drag home & I tire
of the smell of smokestacks, shaved steel.
pocket my hands, they just cold.

—*Jim*

Jim Revisits the South

Postmarked ~ March 27, 1923

It's my absence keeps me
coming back to you.
when apart, how one imagines what is not.
your mouth, uplift
of steel fixed to permanent shape.
your hands store-bought softness.
your voice, no time ticket, teeth punching
shift, or tongue, a foreman threatening
deduction. simply dear, you is sweet,
the rouse of song. when I visit
this once home, might my share
yield a crop daily? melons large
as a moon under whose light men make love
until sleeping. might my ankles twitch
sheepish in pleasure than shake
furiously when I pinned
by my throat & hoisted like rafters
in the hands of summer
storms. when I come home
from a long trip, you always, b,
my welcome. In town, white men will tip
their hats, nod in greeting—
Jim how you been?

—*Jim*

Beatrice Airs Out the House before Jim's Return

Postmarked ~ May 3, 1923

Before you visit, I must set things right.
The fly door unhooked from its hinge,
a napkin folded thick to lengthen a chair's short leg.
How I scrub one room top to bottom,
even baseboards belvedere like clean church shoes.
Wipe fingerprints from water glasses.
I heard word your uncle is salting a heifer,
and men tighten their hotbox
guitar strings for your return.
The North Canadian River might well be drained
the way you take. I suppose you think
in a man's absence, a woman will knead
the callouses from his neck.
From her bedsheets, she smoothed worry.
You traced letters on the insides of my wrists
last time I saw you. I thought your nails welted dahlias
of what we both might call kindness.
Now, I wonder only partially what you wrote:
Survival? A proposal? A Western Railway ticket?
Another woman's name?

An Inventory of Her Blues

Weep for the spilt milk &
Arkansas sweet water.

While setting the brass kettle to cookstove
or water to cool Sear's icebox—

inside weeping crocks of smashed black
clementines, Brer Rabbit Molasses,
Applejack, lard.

Weep for those who hang
like hackberries in locust trees,
their mothers'
washed black dresses & pillbox hats.

For inkwells weeping letters
onto yellow paper North.

Weep for your vanity & neglected
ring finger. Weep as you pick
polyester slips of sweet spire,
dahlias, hyacinths at dusk—

for able men, their spades, rakes, kerosene.

Weep for bread.

Weep for Josephine, Phillis, Harriet
& Gladys.

Go on weeping, at church
onto your blackbird clean shoes,
onto your collar stay, coat lace,
into ringworms of communion wax.

Weep when flushing termites from the wood
ear with vinegar.

When hurling glass, buttons, pennies
at the black dog humming your head, weep,

weep for the rose-breasted grosbeak
& the orioles,
for your nest of scrap
rugs, ribbons & gingham dress ties.

Weep for Greenwood.
For yourself & me, I sure do.

B Contemplates a Reconstructed South

October 19, 1923

Jim. Heaven knows, there isn't no use carrying on
about spilt milk. What things we lose
in the rotgut of harvest—
wet stems   bag
worms suckling fat on fruit
your leaving   or how these days
I remember little of your face.
Each time I tell it   it's just a little
different. What a woman bridges
of blues   suits each one her moods—
over bread   a hurling hum
love-lettered onto yellow paper   scatted
gin at dusk   a pause   to weep
& when she wakes again grinds
toes   wetting the thigh
of some good-looking folks   giggles
do whatever it takes
to mend the renting of her history.
I   woman's   art old as violence.

Beatrice Makes Shadow Puppetry of Jim
on a Sundown Billboard

Sometimes, I feel not much different than the men
that would have you as if wood of black gum dried to break

fast. How I shape you according to my need.
You like a shadow box white

walls. And Jim each time you are something quite different.
Watch the curl of this ring finger— How I might make

quick dog of you, plunging through ryegrass,
long throat bobbing for touch of tooth in my coat.

Watch closely the storyline of my wrist.
Bent a way, how it makes a sundown lover of you—

cowarding your papa's lot as tenant farmer & all them sad
stone fruit trees that border on miles.

In one story, and one story only, I'll concede
I once made a moon of my hands, cupped

its mouth muddy into North Canadian water.
And beside it, an entire billboard lifted, painted lettering

as if to say. Jim: *Have you forgotten? Have you heard
what they do to a man who stands upright?*

I clapped my hands against light, pointed North.
You was brave. Like that you flew away.

No kind of blues that I can sing
seem to soothe or console my mind.
But I have done most everything
that is loving, good, and kind.
Now the man I love, he's a music man
it was my fate to lose.
Now he's forsaken me and gone
With those loving long lost blues.

"Long Lost, Weary Blues" ~ Trixie Smith

Acknowledgments

When we write, we don't write alone. I extend my gratitude to the following individuals and entities who have encouraged, inspired, and helped shape *South Flight* over the past years.

Thank you to my blood kin, admittedly my biggest muse, whose stories I was nursed and grew upon:

To my mama, Audrie Mae, lover of flowers and of the South, who has instilled within me to always hold my head up high in the face of this world's adversities while dressed in my Sunday best. To my papa, Melvin Joseph, visionary, lover of music, my true heart, whose own migration inspired this story and its search of belonging and love. My grandmamas, Charlene Acelene and Galilee Oliphant, whose fire, wisdom, and determination as Black southern women I invocate in every one of these poems. To my sisters, Monica and Shannon, for your unwavering support, for first recognizing me as a poet in those formative years, for your collaboration and friendship.

To my bird, partner, and playmate Micheal Patrick, who has weathered my side during the completion of this project and who has cultivated light, joy, and movement in my darkest creative moments.

To my kin of choice who have lifted me in prayer, community, and joy; I write in conversation to your work and have refined this collection to your careful critiques. When the archive unfolds, I hope we will be cataloged as contemporaries and dear friends like those tender photographs of Jimmy, Nina, and Loraine, who labored art over long-distance calls, porch gardens, and living rooms: Ashanti Anderson, Brenda Delfino, Leelee Jackson, Alicia Mosley, and A. K. Parker.

To my mentor and thesis chair, Allison Hedge Coke, for holding the door open and for seeing the true pulse and music of this manuscript before it was yet *South Flight*.

To the members of the BMFA, Black Light Arts Collective, and Cave Canem, thank-you for providing me a community of Black artists and for your critique even at times when I was both capable and incapable of receiving.

To the models I have fashioned myself and my creative framework after and in conversations with your work: Lucille Clifton, Sadiya Hartman, Alice Walker, Kali Akuno, Ajamu Nangwaya, Clyde Woods, Angela Y. Davis, Toni Morrison, Tyehimba Jess, Tiffany Jeanette King, Frank X Walker, Adrian Matejka, and Zora Neal Hurston.

To the University of California in Riverside for providing me with the opportunity to pursue my Master of Fine Arts in Poetry and providing me the space and resources to put *South Flight* into reality. To Allison Benis White and Katie Ford for serving as my thesis advisors in the early iterations of this project and for the many hours of critique. To Bela Igosa and Katy Gurin and the rest of the UCR poetry workshop, thank-you for your careful feedback, which pushed many of these poems to their fullest potential.

To Ilya Kaminsky for selecting my collection South Flight for the 2021 Georgia Poetry Prize.

To Jon Davies, Elizabeth Adams, Christina Cotter, Erin Kirk, and Beth Snead at UGAPress for your patience and guidance in the production and publication of *South Flight*.

To the editors of the following journals who have made space for *South Flight* and published them in various iterations: *Frontier Poetry, Kweli, POETRY, OklahomaArtFocus, Black Renaissance Noire, Southwestern American Literature, World Literature Today,* the *Pacific Review,* and *Nimrod International Journal.*

To the Black Oklahoma artists, scholars, historians, community organizers, and activists whose work uplifts the histories I have impartially explored in *South Flight* and who continue to do this work nationally and intimately in the Oklahoma community: Najah-Amatullah Hylton, Quraysh Ali Lansana, Shannon Nicole Smith, Skip Hill, Kalenda Eaton, Crystal Z Campbell,

Candace G. Wiley, Clemonce Heard, Hannibal B. Johnson, Marie Casimir, Andre Head and Jessilyn Hall-Head of the Coltrane Group, Sache Primeaux-Shaw, Senator Kevin Matthews, Phetote Mshairi, Jerica Wortham, Mia Wright, the Reverend Dr. Robert Richard Allen Turner, Nkem Ike, and Onikah Asamoa-Caesar, among many others.

To the Oklahoma Historical Society, Greenwood Historical Society, and the Tulsa Historical Society and Museum.

To the Black community of Oklahoma—for your self-determination and resilience in the face of violence.

And always to the endless fortitude and beauty of Black women and our song.

Notes

In "Blacktown Blues of Oklahoma," the lines "against forgetting this home / I call South" were inspired by the title of the anthology *Against Forgetting: Twentieth-Century Poetry of Witness*, edited by Carolyn Forché in 1993.

The parable of the seed referenced in "Jim Waters Makes Parable of Seed" is recounted in Matthew 13:1–9, 18–23.

"*[Greenwood Ghosts Dress Their Sunday Best]*" was inspired by James S. Hirch's *Riot and Remembrance: America's Worst Race Riot and Its Legacy*. Pulling from the history and tradition of resistance of early Black church parades, historian John Hope Franklin who moved to Greenwood in the 1920s described the Sunday afternoons in which the residents of his community would promenade the streets in their Sunday best this way: "It was like pantomime, people moving up and down. They were going in and out of restaurants, and they were just seen to be seen. They were dressed in their finest and they looked beautiful to me."

"[Jim Imagines a Drink with Lead Belly after the Lynching of Lloyd Clay]" alludes to the May 14, 1919, lynching of Lloyd Clay. Twenty-three-year-old Lloyd Clay was dragged from his jail cell by one thousand white men after being falsely accused of raping a white woman. As a crowd of men, women, and children watched, Clay was hung from an elm tree, his body was burned, and a fusillade of bullets were fired into his body. Following the lynching, Clay's family and friends were "cautioned" to keep away from Clay's remains.

In "Beatrice Interprets a Night Terror," the line "what good a dream if I can't interpret it?" is inspired by Langston Hughes's poem "Harlem."

The epigraph for "Jim Recalls the Soldier He Once Was" is from W. E. B. Du Bois, "Returning Soldiers," *The Crisis* 18 (May 1919), 13.

"Beatrice Contemplates the Wild Dog Killing Prey" is based on a May 31, 1921, incident in which mobs of white residents massacred the thriving all-Black neighborhood of Greenwood in Tulsa, Oklahoma. In the days preceding, a common yet deadly trope occurred. Sarah Page, a white woman, falsely accused Dick Rowland, a nineteen-year-old Black man of attempting to sexually assault her on an elevator. Blacks of the Greenwood community took a collective stand of resistance to the mob of white Tulsans that gathered outside the county courthouse. According to witnesses, a white man approached a Black man who was holding an army pistol. After a heated exchange between the two, the white man attempted to grab the pistol from its owner. They struggled and a shot was fired—Black residents were then attacked over a harrowing twenty-four-hour period and their businesses and homes burned to the ground. An estimated three hundred people were killed.

"Love Letter on the Eve of Revolution" and "Beatrice Begs Jim to Pull Out Her Bad Tooth" references Toni Morrison's depiction of the Silent March in her 1993 novel, *Jazz*. On July 28, 1917, ten thousand Black women, men, and children marched down New York's Fifth Avenue to the beat of drums to protest the July 2, 1917, massacre in East Saint Louis, Illinois, that killed dozens of Black residents and left thousands homeless.

"How to Break a Generational Curse (& Other Lessons My Grandmother Has Taught Me)" is dedicated to the wisdom of my grandmothers, Charlene Acelene and Galilee Oliphant.

Italic lines in "For Phillis Wheatley at Water's Edge" are excerpted from various poems by Phillis Wheatley.

"From the Southern Slave Medical Companion" references medical care prescribed for enslaved individuals on southern plantations from various antebellum medical journals and medical manuals as outlined in Glenda Sullivan's "Plantation Medicine and Health Care in the Old South," *Legacy* 10, no. 1 (2010), 17–35, https://opensiuc.lib.siu.edu/legacy/vol10 /iss1/3.

"Drowned & Reborn" is inspired by Clyde Woods's *Development Drowned and Reborn: The Blues and Bourbon Restorations in Post-Katrina New Orleans* (Athens: University of Georgia Press, 2017).

"Zouzou" takes inspiration from the 1927 French film Zouzou, directed by Marc Allégret and starring Josephine Baker. In the film, Baker plays the tragic mulatto Zouzou, who navigates a career of fetishization and spectacle as well as an unrequited love of her white childhood companion, Jean. In the film's finale, Zouzou, clad in only feathers, sings while perched in a gilded birdcage as if an exotic specimen surrounded by the outstretched arms of a white chorus.

Beatrice's interrogation to Jim "You finally flee that terror you claimed?" in "Correspondence from Boley, Oklahoma, to Chicago, Illinois" alludes to Richard Wright's closing lines in part 1 of *Black Boy*: "This was the culture from which I sprang. This was the terror from which I fled."

"Beatrice Reads the Almanac to Forecast the Growing Season": In regions of Oklahoma during summer of 1922, the heat index reached a staggering record high of 116 degrees.

In "[Boley Ghosts Haunt Jim]," the catalog of "*greenwood* & *sulcom*, / *rosewood* & *ocoee*, / *elaine* & *sprinfield* " refers to the racially motivated massacres of Black communities in years leading up to and during the Red Summer of 1919. Founded in 1903 and incorporated in 1905 on Creek freedman Abigail Burnett McCormick's landholdings, Boley, apart from its Cherokee County sibling, Greenwood, was one of the most prosperous and affluent Black towns in Oklahoma during the early 1900s, with more than four thousand citizens and a plethora of businesses, including two banks, three cotton gins, two colleges, an electrical generating plant, a water system, an ice plant, an all Black rodeo, and a Masonic temple. After visiting the town in 1905, Booker T. Washington said of Boley, "It is the most enterprising and, in many ways, the most interesting of the Negro towns in the United States."

"B's Ascension to Bee" is inspired by the Black American folklore popularized by Virginia Hamilton and, later, by Toni Morrison's "The People Could Fly."

"Beatrice & Gladys Bentley Discuss the Fortune of Livin Alone" takes inspiration from queer blues performer Gladys Bentley, who after years serving as a musical pioneer self-renunciated her sexuality in an *Ebony*

87

article titled, "I Am a Woman Again." Gladys, the dethroned Harlem king thrust into the chore of a housewife, wrote, "I inhabited that half-shadow the no-man's-land that existed within the boundary of two sexes. . . . Our number is legion and our heartbreak inconceivable."

"[Jim Imagines He & Charley Patton Pick a Boweavil from Backyard Chicago Crop]" is inspired by Charley Patton's 1928 recording of "Mississippi Boll Weevil Blues." By 1907, all but three counties in the state of Oklahoma cultivated cotton. First documented that same year by Dr. W. D. Hunter in a report to the Oklahoma Agricultural Society, the boll weevil would thereafter expand its stake on the state's most prominent cash crop. By the early 1920s, the boll weevil infestation devoured the northern limit of the cotton belt in the eastern part of the state and alongside other major cotton-growing areas in the American South decimated the industry and livelihood of growers.

"Jim Waters Sweet-Talks Beatrice about the Paradox of Blackness, Our Good Lord & Gold" takes inspiration from Matthew 25:14–30.

"Correspondence from Chicago to Boley" takes inspiration from Genesis 19:26.

"B Contemplates a Reconstructed South" derives influence from Billy Holiday's December 8, 1957, live television performance on CBS's *The Sound of Jazz*. In her introduction to the song "Fine and Mellow," she notes of the fickle nature of the blues, "There's two kinds of blues: there's happy blues and there's sad blues. I don't think I ever sang the same way twice. I don't think I ever sang the same tempo. One night it is a little bit slower, the next it's a little brighter. It's according to how I feel."

THE GEORGIA POETRY PRIZE

Christopher Salerno, *Sun & Urn*

Christopher P. Collins, *My American Night*

Rosa Lane, *Chouteau's Chalk*

Chelsea Dingman, *Through a Small Ghost*

Chioma Urama, *A Body of Water*

Jasmine Elizabeth Smith, *South Flight*